ULTIMATE STICKER BOOK

MARVEL

VILLAINS BEWARE!

HOW TO USE THIS BOOK

Read the captions, then find the sticker
that best fits in the space.
(Hint: check the sticker labels for clues!)

•

Don't forget that your stickers can be
stuck down and peeled off again.

•

There are lots of fantastic extra stickers too!

LONDON, NEW YORK,
MELBOURNE, MUNICH AND DELHI

Written by Rahul Ganguly

Edited by Emma Grange, Shari Last,
Garima Sharma and Chitra Subramanyam

Designed by Neha Ahuja, Karan Chaudhary,
Guy Harvey and Lauren Rosier

Jacket designed by Karan Chaudhary

First published in Great Britain in 2014 by
Dorling Kindersley Limited,
80 Strand, London WC2R 0RL
A Penguin Random House Company

10 9 8 7 6 5 4 3 2 1
001—253664—Mar/14

All rights reserved. No part of this publication may be reproduced, stored
in a retrieval system or transmitted in any form or by any means, electronic,
mechanical, photocopying, recording or otherwise, without the prior
written permission of the copyright owner.

A CIP catalogue for this book is available from the British Library.

ISBN: 978-1-40934-904-4

Colour reproduction by Alta Image Ltd, UK
Printed and bound by L-Rex Printing Co., Ltd, China

Discover more at
www.dk.com
www.marvel.com

© 2014 MARVEL

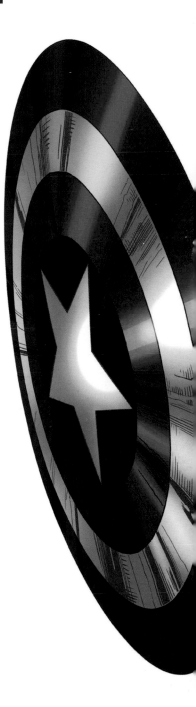

SUPER HEROES

When villains attack, Super Heroes from across the universe will come to the rescue. Whether they swing from rooftops, fly through the air or bound over skyscrapers, these brave heroes will do everything in their power to defeat evil!

SPIDER-MAN
Spider-Man is a fearless crime fighter who swings across New York City on his web. He catches villains with his super-fast reflexes.

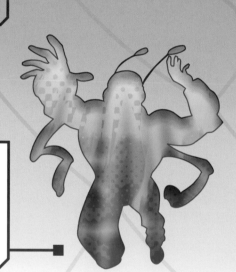

ANT-MAN
Ant-Man shrinks to a tiny size to fight crime. His small body lets him sneak up on criminals without being caught.

DAREDEVIL
Daredevil is blind, but he has an amazing sense of hearing and smell. He uses his sharp senses to defend against even the fastest enemy attacks!

WOLVERINE
An unbreakable metal covers this Super Hero's skeleton and protects him. Wolverine's strong bones and sharp claws make him almost unstoppable in combat.

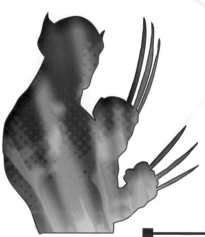

IRON FIST
Beware the punch of Iron Fist! This hero uses an energy called chi to become super-strong and battle his enemies.

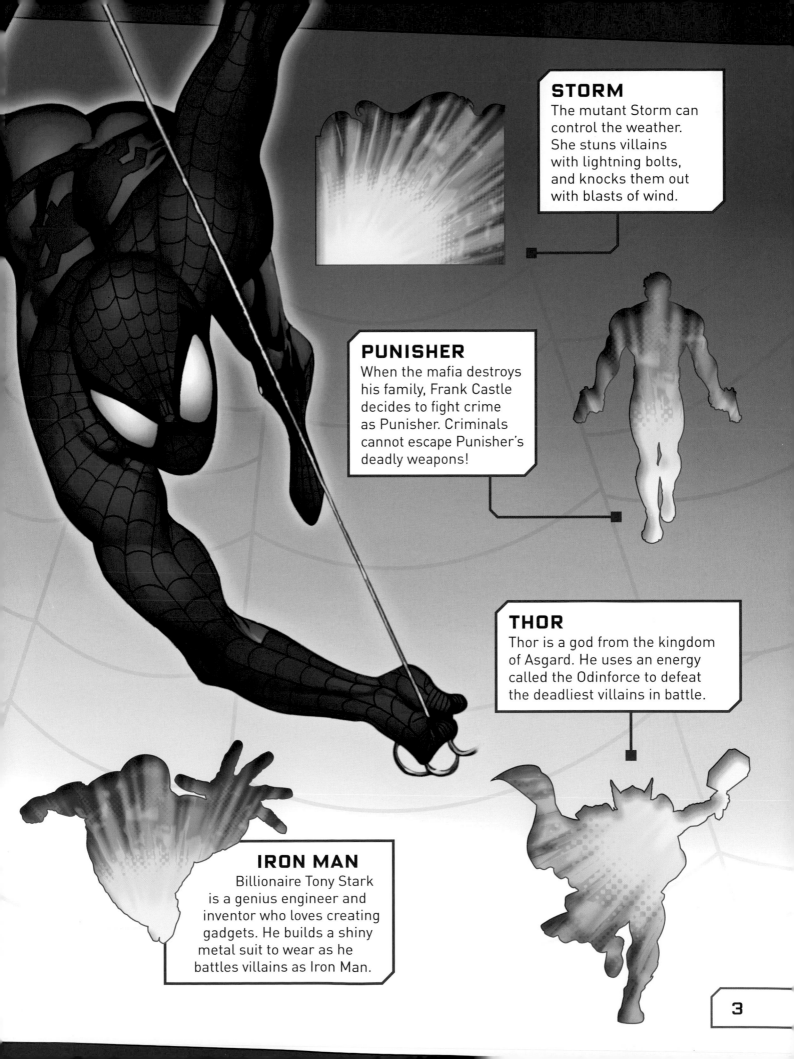

STORM

The mutant Storm can control the weather. She stuns villains with lightning bolts, and knocks them out with blasts of wind.

PUNISHER

When the mafia destroys his family, Frank Castle decides to fight crime as Punisher. Criminals cannot escape Punisher's deadly weapons!

THOR

Thor is a god from the kingdom of Asgard. He uses an energy called the Odinforce to defeat the deadliest villains in battle.

IRON MAN

Billionaire Tony Stark is a genius engineer and inventor who loves creating gadgets. He builds a shiny metal suit to wear as he battles villains as Iron Man.

EVIL VILLAINS

Villains come in all shapes and sizes, from sinister humans to vicious aliens. Some disguise themselves and pretend to be good, while others are proud to be bad. But they all want to succeed in their evil plans to conquer or destroy. Can anybody stop them?

DOCTOR DOOM
This sorcerer rules the kingdom of Latveria, but wants to take over Earth! Doctor Doom destroys his enemies with energy bolts.

KANG
Kang is a time traveller who wants to control Earth and its people. His suit can survive any kind of energy attack.

DORMAMMU
A creature made of fiery energy, Dormammu wants to rule the world. He has flames shooting out of his head!

LOKI
Loki is the mischievous son of Odin, the king of Asgard. Loki is jealous of his step-brother, Thor, and wants to rule Asgard on his own.

SANDMAN
The criminal Sandman can turn his body into grains of sand. Watch out Spider-Man – this villain can easily slip through your fingers!

WHIPLASH

When angry Russian scientist Whiplash is around, trouble is not far behind. Beware his electric whips. They can slice through almost anything!

KINGPIN

Kingpin controls a massive criminal network. His super-heavy muscles and scheming mind make him a deadly foe in combat.

JUGGERNAUT

Once the immense Juggernaut starts running, nothing will stop him. He can slam through anything and anyone in his way!

APOCALYPSE

Apocalypse believes that only the strongest should be allowed to survive. He thinks humans are weak, and has tried to destroy Earth many times.

INCREDIBLE POWERS

Some heroes can fly, some are super-strong, while others can blast their foes with energy. Heroes can train hard to develop fighting skills, but it's super powers that give them their edge. Can energy beams defeat defence shields? Is flight better than magic? Which super power is the best?

BEAM BLASTER
Watch out! Cyclops blasts solar beams from his eyes. He cannot control the beams, and has to wear a special visor all the time.

SELF-HEALING
Wolverine can heal himself from almost any injury in seconds. This makes it almost impossible to defeat him in a fight.

ANCIENT MAGIC
Stephen Strange is the most powerful magician in the world. He uses a mysterious energy to cast spells and defeat mighty foes.

SHOCKER
Wasp can shrink to a tiny size and grow wings to fly. She zaps villains with electric bolts. Bzzzt!

FLYING HIGH
Falcon can talk to birds. He uses this ability to track criminals from the sky. He wears a suit that helps him fly really fast.

SUPER STRETCH
Leader of the Fantastic Four, Mr Fantastic is a scientist with a super-stretchy body. The springy hero can wrap himself around enemies to trap them.

BRUTE STRENGTH
The mutant Beast looks like a gigantic blue bear and has enormous physical strength. Beast can destroy villains with his bare hands.

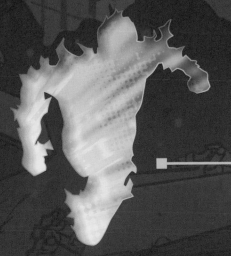

FIREPOWER
Flaming hero Human Torch can cover himself in fire. He can fling massive fireballs at villains and gives them a scorching time.

SUPER SOLDIER

Not everyone is born with special powers. Captain America was once an ordinary man called Steven Rogers. But a secret experiment turned him into a mighty Super Hero. Cap served in the U.S. Army, and also led the Avengers super team on many missions.

STRONG

Captain America is one of the strongest humans ever. He can lift up to twice his body weight, and run for miles before getting tired.

MIGHTY SHIELD

Cap's enemies are terrified of his shield. By throwing it, Cap can knock out many villains at once. Watch out!

WINTER SOLDIER

Cap's pal Bucky Barnes turned evil and became the Winter Soldier. Cap had to choose whether to fight the Winter Soldier or save his friend!

OUT COLD

When his plane crashed in a freezing ocean, Cap was trapped in ice. The Avengers found the crash site many years later, and rescued the frozen hero.

SWORN ENEMY

Nazi agent Red Skull is Cap's most dangerous foe. This red-headed villain can destroy his enemies with a deadly chemical called "red dust".

USE YOUR EXTRA
STICKERS TO
CREATE YOUR
OWN SCENE.

SUPER TEAMS

Defeating the deadliest villains in the universe is no easy task. Sometimes a threat is so great that heroes unite! With combined super powers, battle experience and courage, a team of Super Heroes is sure to strike fear in the heart of every villain!

AVENGERS
The Avengers are one of the longest serving Super Hero teams ever. They defend Earth from attacks by deadly villains.

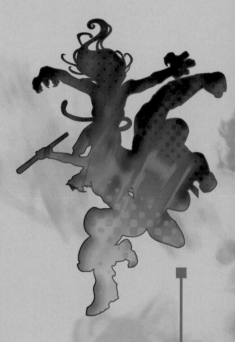

INVADERS
Fiery crime-fighter Blazing Skull formed the Invaders with U.S. Agent and Union Jack to protect the world from Nazi attacks.

WEST COAST AVENGERS
When the Avengers expand their operations, they recruit heroes to serve as a branch on the West Coast of America.

ATLANTEANS
Atlanteans are warriors who live in the underwater kingdom of Atlantis. These deep-sea dwellers are ten times stronger than ordinary humans.

X-MEN

A group of good mutants called the X-Men protect Earth from evil mutants. They have unique powers, thanks to a special x-gene in their bodies.

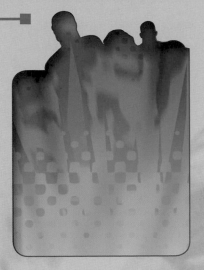

FANTASTIC FOUR

The Fantastic Four are Invisible Woman, The Thing, Human Torch and Mr Fantastic. They gain super powers after getting blasted with radiation.

ASGARDIANS

The Asgardians are super-powered gods from the floating kingdom of Asgard. They protect Earth from villains of other worlds.

CLOAK AND DAGGER

Best buddies Cloak and Dagger fight criminals together. Dagger stuns villains with light, while Cloak traps them in a dimension of darkness.

AWESOME SUITS

A super suit can help Super Heroes do incredible things. Suits can enhance heroes' powers or give them extra abilities. They can help heroes soar through the skies, turn invisible or even deflect bullets. A fearsome costume can even help scare foes during battle!

JET POWER
Iron Man's suit can control any computer in the world. It also has air jets that help him fly.

SOLDIER'S GARB
Cap wears a red, white and blue suit that looks like the American flag. The armoured suit protects him from bullets.

SPIDER SUIT
Spider-Man's super-stretchy costume helps him swing across the city with ease. He also has a secret belt for his gadgets and tools.

FLIGHT GEAR
Falcon uses wings of light attached to his suit to fly really fast. The super-tough suit is also bulletproof.

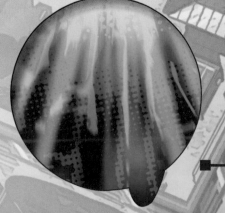

VANISHING ACT
Invisible Woman's outfit is made of material that turns invisible along with her. It can also transmit her location to her teammates.

USE YOUR EXTRA
STICKERS TO
CREATE YOUR
OWN SCENE.

ALIENS

Earth's heroes have encountered many aliens on their adventures. These beings from other worlds sometimes help Super Heroes battle wicked villains. But there are evil aliens too – and they have their own sinister plans to rule the galaxy!

SILVER SURFER

Silver Surfer often teams up with Earth's Super Heroes. He is powered by a mysterious alien force, which increases his strength and helps him fly through space.

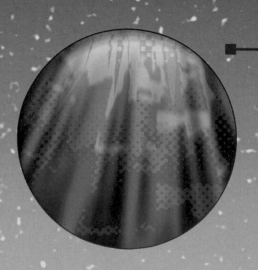

CHITAURI

Wicked shape-shifters called the Chitauri love creating trouble. They once teamed up with the evil Loki to defeat the Avengers and take over Earth.

SKRULLS

Skrulls are a race of evil aliens who can change their appearance to look like anyone. They are the main enemies of the Kree.

SYMBIOTE

This mysterious villain once fused with Spider-Man, turning him evil. Spidey had a tough time freeing himself from Symbiote.

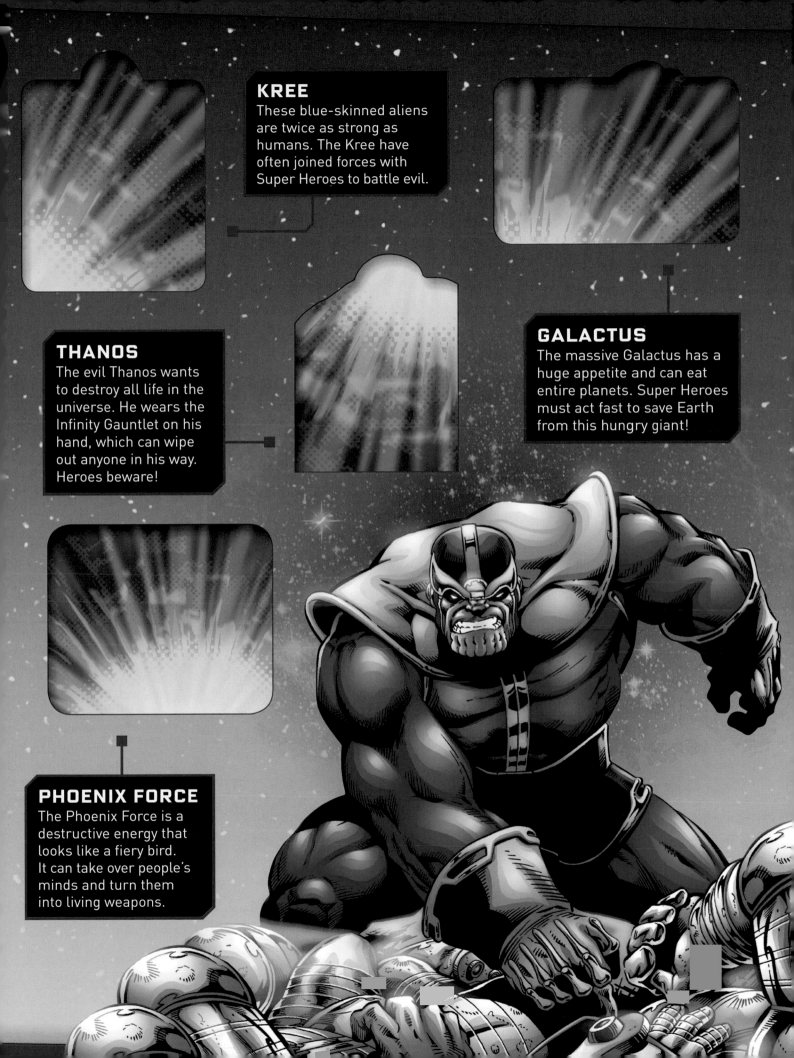

KREE
These blue-skinned aliens are twice as strong as humans. The Kree have often joined forces with Super Heroes to battle evil.

GALACTUS
The massive Galactus has a huge appetite and can eat entire planets. Super Heroes must act fast to save Earth from this hungry giant!

THANOS
The evil Thanos wants to destroy all life in the universe. He wears the Infinity Gauntlet on his hand, which can wipe out anyone in his way. Heroes beware!

PHOENIX FORCE
The Phoenix Force is a destructive energy that looks like a fiery bird. It can take over people's minds and turn them into living weapons.

ROBOTS AND CYBORGS

In the battle of good versus evil, robots and cyborgs also have to decide which side they are on. Robots are machines that can think on their own, and cyborgs are people with robot parts inside them. They have the power to help or to destroy. Which path will they choose?

DOCTOR OCTOPUS
The cyborg Doctor Octopus is one of Spider-Man's deadliest foes. He uses robotic arms strapped to his body to attack people.

ULTRON
A metal robot called Ultron turned evil when his programming became faulty. He can control people's minds to make them obey his orders.

NEBULA
This greedy cyborg wants to rule the universe. Nebula can change her appearance by using a cyborg device inside her body.

VISION
Ultron built a biomechanical being called Vision, who was programmed to be evil. But Vision decides to become an Avenger and protect the world.

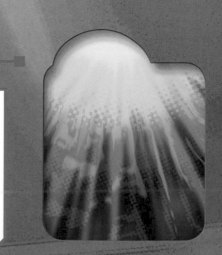

Strong

God of Thunder

Super Punch

Kree

Dormammu

Ancient Magic

Spider Suit

Green Rage

Spidey

Master
Archer

Chitauri

**West Coast
Avengers**

Wolverine

Sworn Enemy

Kang

Flight Gear

Machine Hero

Nebula

Iron Man

Thanos

Firepower

Avengers

Power Throw

Flying Kick

Fantastic Four

Storm

Skrulls

Jet Power

Mighty Shield

Flying High

Team Meeting

Super Aim

Iron Fist

Kingpin

Shield Throw

Green Hero

Evil Doom

Atlanteans

Ultron

Silver Surfer

Vanishing Act

Shocker

Invaders

Leaping Hero

Apocalypse

Mighty Thor

Widow's Punch

Mighty Hero

Unstoppable Thing

Out Cold

Vision

Doctor Octopus

Winter Soldier

Jet Speed

Soldier's Garb

Spider-Man

Secret Spy

Sharp Claws

Fearless Soldier

Silver Hero

Beam Blaster

Thor's Charge

Smash!

Symbiote

Whiplash

Anger

High Flyer

Daredevil

Self-healing

Loki

Web Slinger

Brute Strength

X-Men

Punisher

Fearless God

On Target

War Hero

Juggernaut

Hulk Attack

Galactus

Asgardians

Ant-Man

Sandman

Super Stretch

Thor

Deadly Spy

Green Giant

Doctor Doom

Phoenix Force

Cloak and Dagger